SPOT

COMMUNITY HELPERS

FARMERS

by Golriz Golkar

amicus LEARNING

milk

coop

Look for these words and pictures as you read.

tractor

crops

Farmers are good helpers.
What do they do?

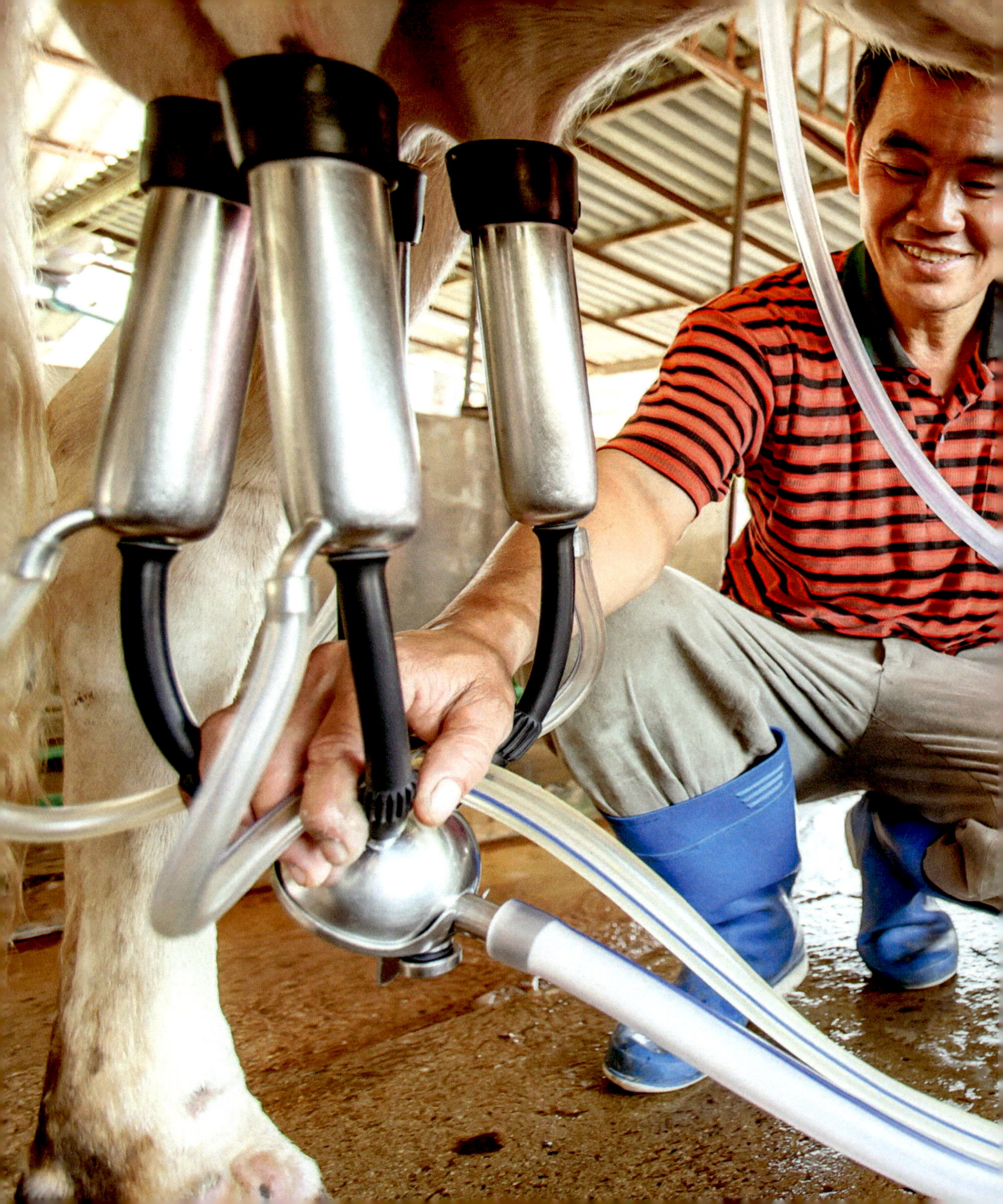

A farmer milks his cows.

Moo!

He sells the milk.

milk

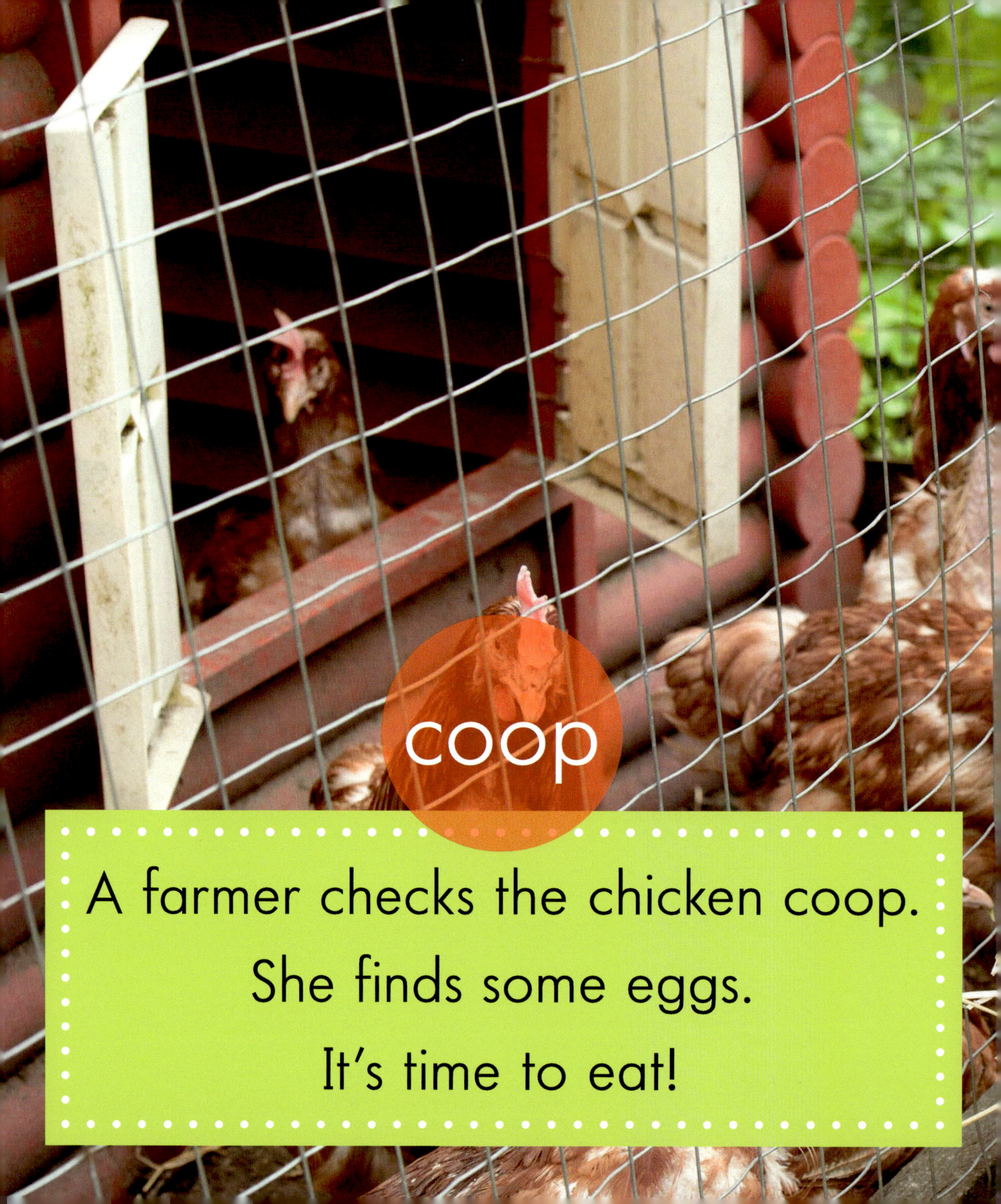

coop

A farmer checks the chicken coop.
She finds some eggs.
It's time to eat!

A farmer drives a tractor.

Humm!

He plants seeds.

tractor

crops

Here is a field.
A farmer grows crops.
Corn will grow here.

This farmer works in a fruit orchard.
She picks pears off the trees.
Yum!

Farmers grow food we need.
They make our lives better!

milk

coop

Did you find?

tractor

crops

Spot is published by Amicus Learning, an imprint of Amicus
P.O. Box 227, Mankato, MN 56002
www.amicuspublishing.us

Library of Congress Cataloging-in-Publication Data
Names: Golkar, Golriz, author.
Title: Farmers / by Golriz Golkar.
Description: Mankato, MN : Amicus Learning, an imprint of Amicus, [2026] | Series: Spot community helpers | Audience: Ages 4–7 | Audience: Grades K–1 | Summary: "Farmers grow our food, raise cattle, and more. Learn how they help the community in this low-level beginning reader that reinforces new vocabulary with a search-and-find feature. A great early social studies book that will inspire kindergartners and first graders to learn about jobs in their community"— Provided by publisher.
Identifiers: LCCN 2024043693 (print) | LCCN 2024043694 (ebook) | ISBN 9798892004893 (library binding) | ISBN 9798892005432 (paperback) | ISBN 9798892005975 (ebook)
Subjects: LCSH: Farmers—Juvenile literature. | Farm life—Juvenile literature.
Classification: LCC S519 .G63 2026 (print) | LCC S519 (ebook) | DDC 630—dc23/eng/20241228
LC record available at https://lccn.loc.gov/2024043693
LC ebook record available at https://lccn.loc.gov/2024043694

Ana Brauer, editor
Deb Miner, series designer
Sara Hood, book designer and photo researcher

Photos by Alamy Stock Photo/Wavebreakmedia Ltd IP-240425, cover; Getty Images/ArtistGNDphotography, 10–11, filmstudio, 12–13, ProfessionalStudioImages, 3; Shutterstock/BearFotos, 14, Ljupco Smokovski, 1, Olexandr Panchenko, 6–7, Tanes Ngamsom, 4–5, Valentin Valkov, 8–9